Homework Helpers
Eng

CW01583285

Ages 7
Key Stage 2 / Year 3

Alan Gardiner

Longman
An imprint of Pearson Education
Harlow, England · London · New York · Reading, Massachusetts · San Francisco
Toronto · Don Mills, Ontario · Sydney · Tokyo · Singapore · Hong Kong · Seoul
Taipei · Cape Town · Madrid · Mexico City · Amsterdam · Munich · Paris · Milan

Series editors:

Stuart Wall & Geoff Black

With thanks to Val Mitchell for additional material and Heather Ancient for editorial development work

A complete range of **Homework Helpers** is available.

		ENGLISH	MATHS	SCIENCE
Key Stage 1	Ages 5–6 Year 1	✓	✓	Science is not included in the National Tests at Key Stage 1
	Ages 6–7 Year 2	✓	✓	
Key Stage 2	Ages 7–8 Year 3	✓	✓	✓
	Ages 8–9 Year 4	✓	✓	✓
	Ages 9–10 Year 5	✓	✓	✓
	Ages 10–11 Year 6	✓	✓	✓

Pearson Education Limited
Edinburgh Gate, Harlow
Essex CM20 2JE, England
and Associated Companies throughout the world

First published 2000

British Library Cataloguing in Publication Data
A catalogue entry for this title is available from the British Library

ISBN 0-582-38144-4

Printed in Great Britain by Henry Ling Ltd, at the Dorset Press, Dorchester, Dorset

This is for grown-ups!

Guidance and advice

Schools are now asked to set regular homework, even for young children. Government guidelines for Year 3 (ages 7–8) suggest $1\frac{1}{2}$ hours of homework a week. Children are also encouraged to do at least 10–20 minutes of reading each day.

The Numeracy Hour

The daily Literacy Hour was introduced into schools in September 1999. During this session, teachers focus on three broad areas: word, sentence and text. The aim of the Literacy Hour is to develop a child's reading and writing skills.

All the activities in this book are written to complement the Literacy Hour. The emphasis is on short, enjoyable exercises designed to stimulate a child's interest in language. Each activity will take 10–20 minutes, depending on the topic, and the amount of writing and drawing.

Themes and topics

Throughout the book key words have been set in **bold** text – these highlight the themes and content of the activities, and provide a guide to the topics covered.

Encourage your child

Leave your child to do the activity on their own, but be available to answer any questions. Try using phrases like: That's a good idea! How do you think you could do it? What happens if you do it this way? These will encourage your child to think about how they could answer the question for themselves.

If your child is struggling ...

Younger children might need help understanding the question before they try to work out an answer, and children who need help with reading or writing may need you to work with them. If your child is struggling with the writing, ask them to find the answer and then write it in for them. Remember even if your child gets stuck, be sure to tell them they are doing well.

The activities start on the next page! Have you got your pens and pencils ready?

Check the answers together

When they have done all they can, sit down with them and go through the answers together. Check they have not misunderstood any important part of the activity. If they have, try to show them why they are going wrong. Ask them to explain what they have done, right or wrong, so that you can understand how they are thinking.

You will find answers to the activities at the back of this book. You can remove the last page if you think your child might look at the answers before trying an activity. Sometimes there is no set answer because your child has been asked for their own ideas. Check that your child's answer is appropriate and shows they have understood the question.

Be positive!

If you think your child needs more help with a particular topic try to think of some similar but easier examples. You don't have to stick to the questions in the book – ask your own: Did you like that? Can you think of any more examples? Have a conversation about the activity. Be positive, giving praise for making an effort and understanding the question, not just getting the right answers. Your child should enjoy doing the activities and at the same time discover that learning is fun.

More on Spelling

Help your child to keep a list of words that they tend to spell incorrectly. Encourage your child to use these words regularly in their own writing, so as to get into the habit of spelling them correctly. Help your child break down words into separate sounds or syllables ('home-work', 'read-ing'). This makes the spelling and reading of unfamiliar words easier.

Children can test themselves in the following way:

Look at the word

Say the spelling out loud

Cover the word so they can't see it

Write it down

Check that it's spelt correctly

Poems, songs and nursery rhymes can help with a child's spellings because they encourage children to develop an awareness of sound patterns and an understanding of the link between sounds and letters.

Getting to know you

Tell us all about yourself!

Fill in the answers to these questions.

Name ______________________________

Address ______________________________

____

____

Age __________ years __________ months

The name of my school is ______________________________

____

My favourite colour is ______________________________

My favourite food is ______________________________

My favourite drink is ______________________________

My best friend's name is ______________________________

I live with ______________________________

Plurals

Nouns often have an *s* added to make them **plural**. Nouns which end in s, ss, sh, ch, x or z need es to make them plural.

Add s or es to make these nouns plural.

fox	push
bench	zoo
coach	wish
grass	box
gas	drink
smile	fizz
sock	bath

Now think of some other words that need es to make them plural.

Similar words

Sort these words into pairs of words with similar meanings.
One pair has been done for you.

country enquire ask lofty
cheerful sad pretty wrong
happy tall complete nation
attractive miserable incorrect whole

cheerful	happy

Find the nouns

Look at these words. Draw a circle round the words that are **nouns**. You should be able to find ten.

Nouns tell us the names of people, places and things.

slowly
beautiful
astronaut
saucer
yellow
funny
sing
new
computer
red
Wendy
hurry
squeeze
house
London
crowded
penguin
zoo
walked
aeroplane
old
grass

Write your own list of words that are nouns: ____________________

____

____

Word hunt

Here are some words that use different letters to make the same **vowel sound**:

her bird word fur stirred were heard purr

These words are all hidden in the puzzle below.

To find them you need to look down and across.

h	e	r	n	a	r	b	s
m	p	r	m	c	n	i	t
w	u	u	o	g	d	r	i
e	r	h	e	a	r	d	r
r	r	c	k	i	f	u	r
e	h	u	z	s	s	b	e
b	t	m	s	w	o	r	d

Changing words

Turn one word into another one by changing one letter at a time.

The first one has been done for you.

1

bed
bad
sad
sat

2

oat
____
____
bin

3

dog
____
____
cat

4

time
____
____
lamp

5

seed
____
____
bent

6

cake
____
____
line

7

pen
____
____
hat

8

wind
____
____
bald

9

walk
____
____
tile

Make up your own changing word games.

Getting it right!

Add **ing** to the ends of these words. One has been done for you.

If the word ends in e, drop the e when you add ing.

1. climb + ing = climbing
2. have + ing = ________
3. make + ing = ________
4. laugh + ing = ________
5. call + ing = ________
6. take + ing = ________
7. snow + ing = ________
8. rain + ing = ________
9. try + ing = ________
10. smile + ing = ________

Dictionary quiz

A **dictionary** tells us what words mean. We can also use a dictionary to check the spellings of words.

Usually a dictionary also tells us which words are nouns, verbs, adjectives and so on. Here are some words from a dictionary. Answer the questions about them.

The word crash doesn't always have the same meaning, so the different meanings are numbered.

The words in a dictionary are arranged in alphabetical order.

crash *noun* **1** a sudden loud noise; **2** a violent vehicle accident; **3** a sudden failure of a computer or a computer program; **crash** *verb*

crawl *verb* to move slowly with your body close to the ground, or on your hands and knees

cried *see* CRY

crime *noun* something that is wrong and can be punished by law; **criminal** *noun*

^{1}**crisp** *adjective* **1** hard and dry; easily broken; **2** firm; fresh; **crispy** *adjective*

^{2}**crisp** *noun* a thin piece of potato cooked in hot fat, dried, and sold in packets

The word crisp is sometimes an adjective, sometimes a noun.

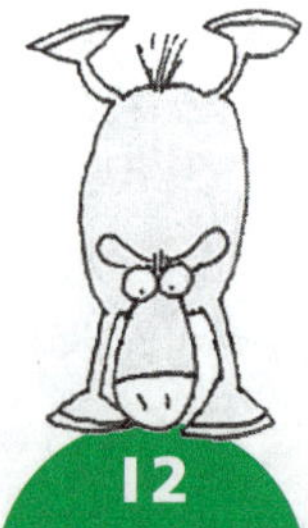

1 Is the word crime a noun, verb or adjective?

____

2 How many different meanings does the word crash have?

____

3 Which other word would you look up to find the meaning of the word cried?

____

4 On this dictionary page, some words have been left out. They all come between crawl and cried. If you have a dictionary, see how many of the missing words you can find and write them down here.

____

____

5 Here are some more words beginning with the letters cr. If you were writing a dictionary, how would you explain their meanings? Write in your answers, then compare them with the explanations in a real dictionary if you can.

crowd ______________________________

____

crown ______________________________

____

crumb ______________________________

____

Writing a diary

These pictures show what Sally did when she had a week's holiday from school. Imagine you are Sally and you are writing a diary. Write what happened on each day in the space on the page opposite. One day has been filled in already.

MONDAY

I went to the zoo.
I saw elephants
and lots of other
animals.

TUESDAY

WEDNESDAY

THURSDAY

FRIDAY

Why not write your own diary for a week?

You could draw some pictures of the things that happen to you!

Find the verbs

Draw a circle round each of the **verbs** in this jumble of words. You should find ten.

Verbs are often 'doing' words.

large fast

freezer

sew

listen

hunter

find swim

collect

draw school news

young

green grow juggle

swimmer ask

throw

What have you done today? Write your own sentences and underline the verbs.

Past and present

Fill in the gaps to complete the pairs of **present tense** and **past tense** verbs. One has been done for you.

Here's a sentence with past tense verbs: 'Yesterday I ***found*** *Sarah's sweets and* ***ate*** *them all!'*

Here's a sentence with a present tense verb: 'Now I ***keep*** *my sweets in a secret place.'*

1	catch	caught
2	see	
3		thought
4	keep	
5	throw	
6		went
7		knew
8	grow	
9	wake	
10		did

In other words ...

A **thesaurus** groups together words and phrases that have similar meanings.

On this page you can see the other words you might find if you looked up the words road, flap and lamp.

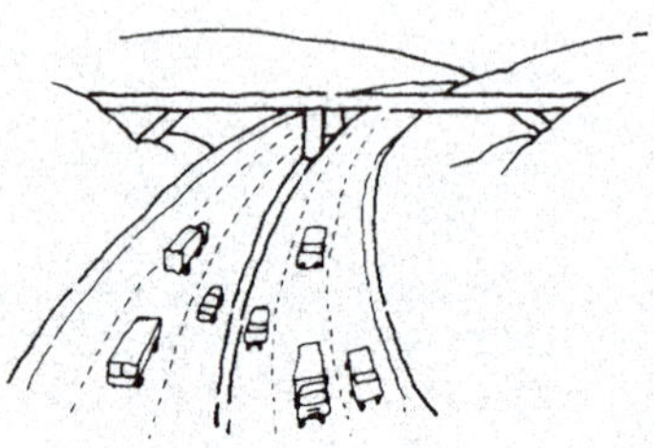

motorway

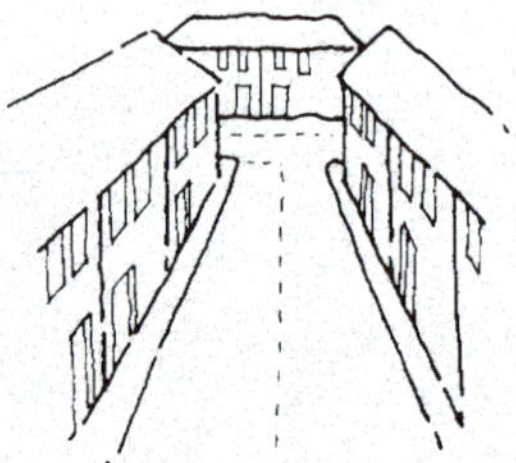

street

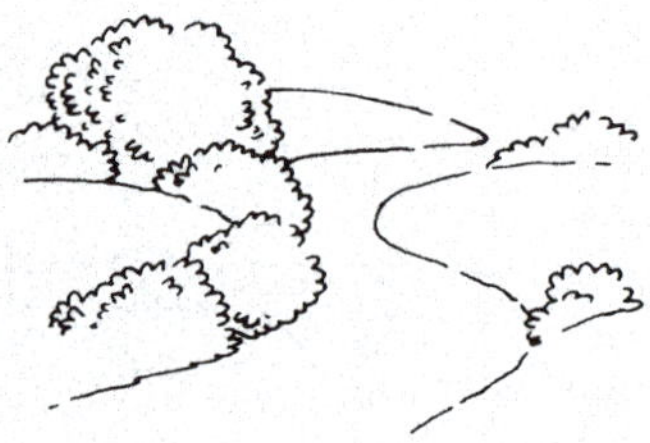

lane

catflap

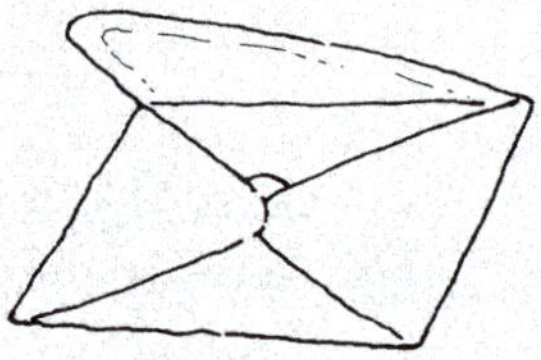

envelope flap

window shutter

pumpkin lantern

table lamp

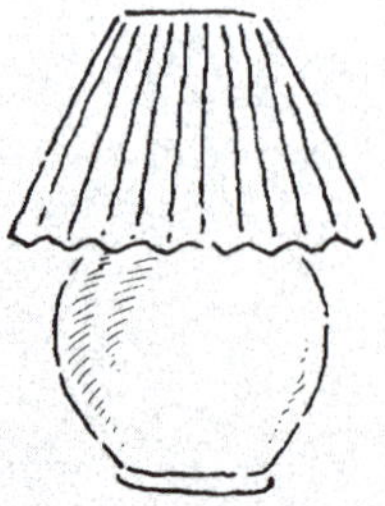

desk lamp

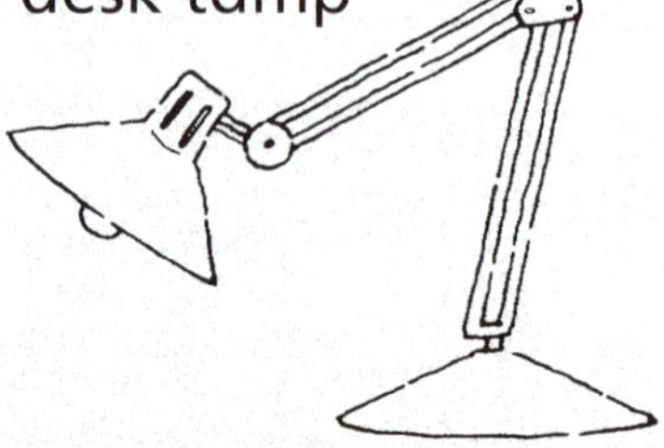

1 How many different words for road are shown in the thesaurus?

2 Which type of road is for cars, coaches and lorries, but not for people to walk on?

3 What type of road has houses and shops along it?

4 What kind of flap do you stick down?

5 What kind of flap is often built into a door?

6 What are the different types of lamp shown in the thesaurus?

7 What kind of lamp would you find near a bed?

8 When would you see a pumpkin lantern?

Beginnings …

Here are some **prefixes**:

Prefixes are groups of letters found at the beginnings of words.

pre
re
anti
dis
mis
non

Choose prefixes from this list to put in front of the words.

1 The magician showed us a rabbit, then made it ________ appear.

2 'You didn't do that very well, did you? I think you had better ________ do it!'

3 I turned the key ________ clockwise and the door opened.

4 I thought he was talking ________ sense.

5 Dinosaurs roamed the earth in ________ historic times.

6 I can't find my pencil case. I must have ________ placed it.

*A prefix usually means the same thing every time it's used. For instance, **pre** normally means **before**.*

Can you work out the meaning of any of the other prefixes on this page?

... and endings

Here are three **suffixes**:

ly	ful	less

Suffixes are groups of letters found at the ends of words.

The first one has been done for you.

Complete the table below by adding each of these suffixes to the words shown. If the suffix can't be added to the word to make a new word, put X.

	ly	ful	less
use	✘	useful	useless
sad			
proud			
hope			
quick			
slow			
nice			
head			
loud			
care			
clear			

You can add 'ly' to useful to make usefully. Does this work with any of the other words?

Missing letters

Did you know that *haven't* is a short version of *have not?* Can you match up the other pairs like this? Colour each pair using a different colour.

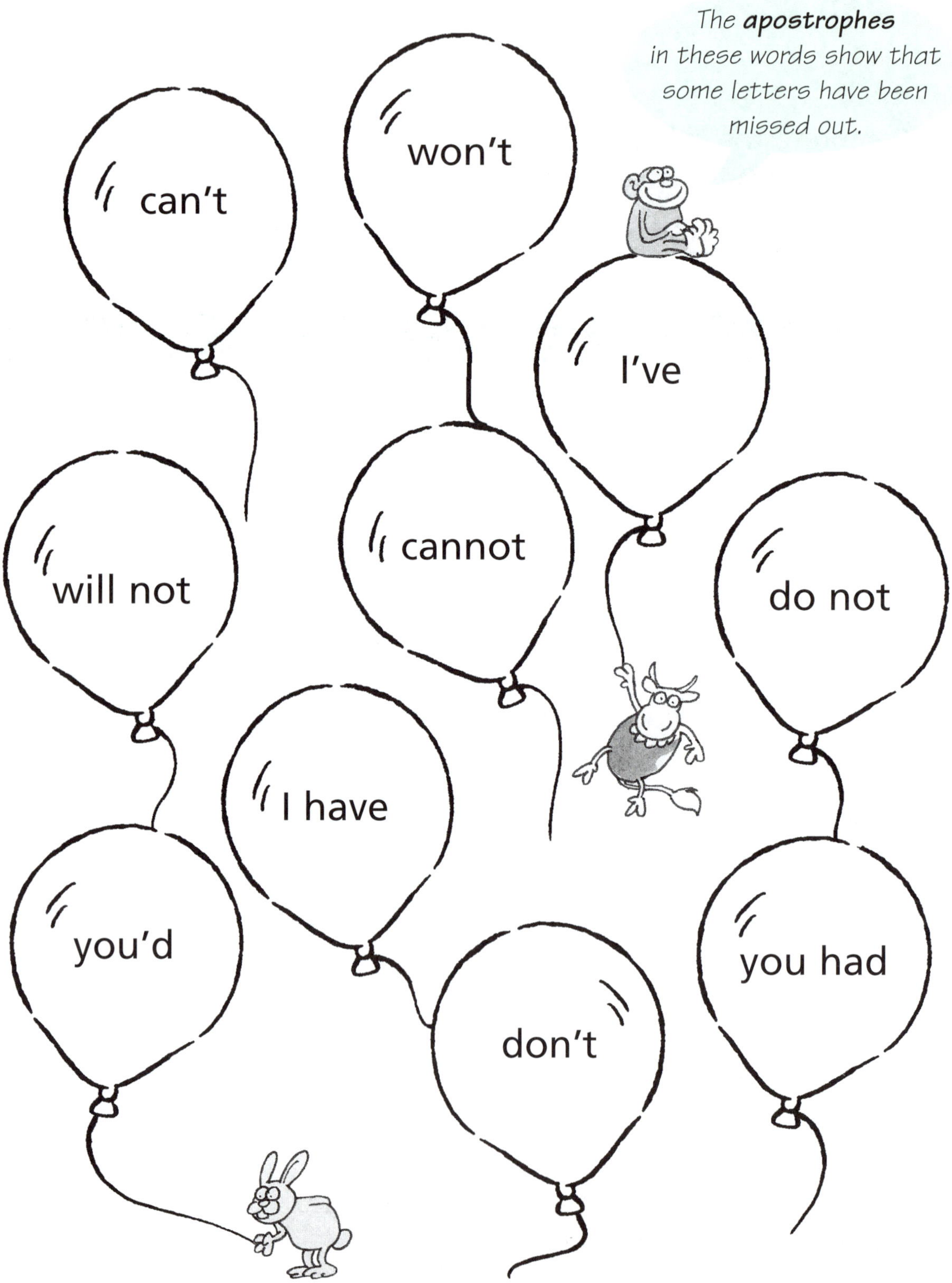

Joining words

Find a word to fit each picture by joining two of the words shown in the middle. One has been done for you.

Words that are joined like this are called ***compound words.***

1

playground

2

3

4

5

6

foot

basket

print

shoe

air

play

port

mill

ground

ball

wind

lace

Find the meaning

On the left are some words from a **dictionary**. On the right are their meanings, but they are in the wrong order. Draw lines to join each word to its correct meaning.

tower	1 a hard covering to protect the head, worn by soldiers, policemen etc.
stream	2 a liquid cooked food often containing small pieces of meat, fish or vegetables
hat	3 a tall building standing alone or forming part of a castle, church etc.
invite	4 a covering placed on top of the head
soup	5 a natural flow of water, smaller than a river
helmet	6 to ask somebody to do something or go somewhere, such as to a party

Opposites

I'm ***up.***

Sort these words into pairs of **opposites**.
One pair has been done for you.

Opposite words are called ***antonyms.***

I'm ***down.***

short

rude

nice

over

polite

cold

lower

tall

upper

under

nasty

hot

hot	cold		

Alphabetical order

Tony is helping out for the day in a video shop. He has to put some films in **alphabetical order**. Can you help him sort out the eight titles below? The first one has been done for you.

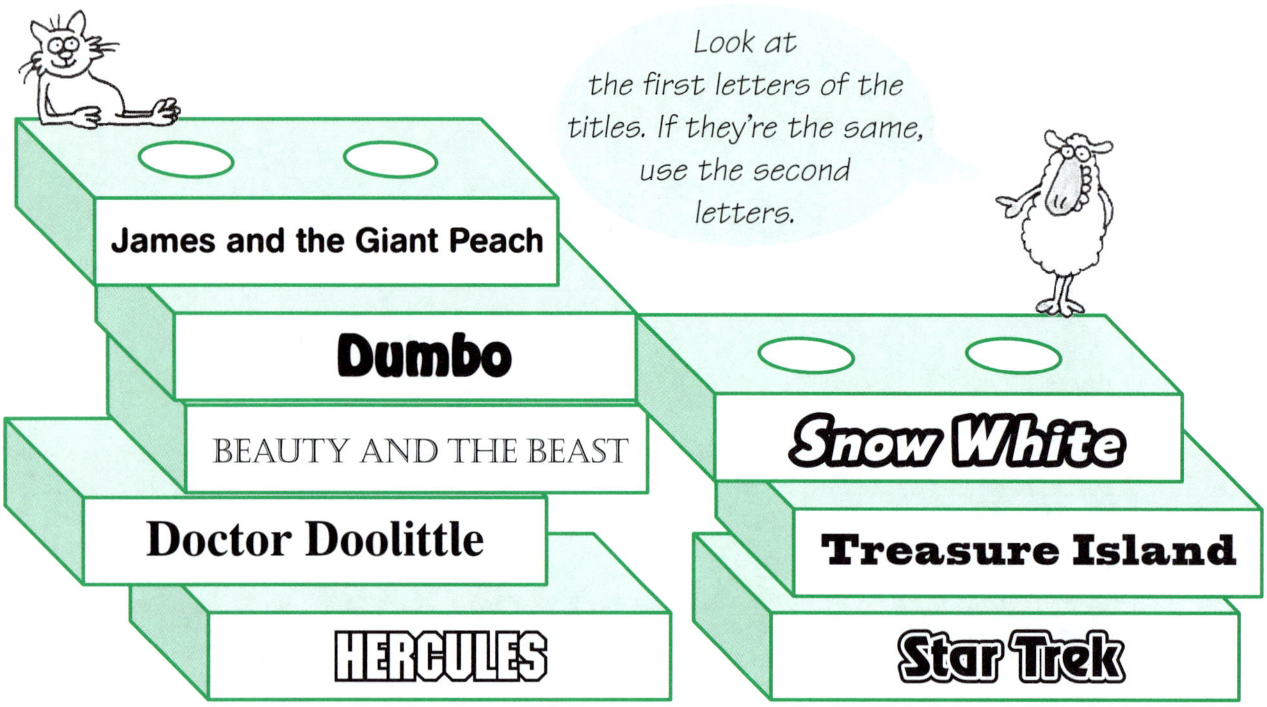

1 Beauty and the Beast

2 ______________________

3 ______________________

4 ______________________

5 ______________________

6 ______________________

7 ______________________

8 ______________________

Secret code

Jodie has sent Max a secret message.

If you write the rest of the alphabet in the bottom boxes, you can decode the message.

The top letters are the code letters and the bottom ones are the real letters.

a	b	c	d	e	f	g	h	i	j
b	c	d	e						

k	l	m	n	o	p	q	r	s	t

u	v	w	x	y	z
					a

The first word is done for you.

Now work out what Jodie's message means.

Sgd	rvddsr	zqd	adghmc	sgd
The	______	______	______	______
bknbj.	Dzs	sghr	ldrrzfd	vgdm
______	______	______	______	______
xnt	gzud	qdzc	hs!	
______	______	______	______	

Make your own code by moving the alphabet along two, three or more places.

Months and days

Nicki is making a **calendar**. You can help her by filling in the missing letters in the months of the year.

Jan ___ ___ ry

J ___ ___ e

Ap ___ ___ l

Ju ___ y

D ___ ___ ___ ___ ber

O ___ ___ ___ ber

Feb ___ ___ ___ ___ y

M ___ ___ ___ h

M ___ y

A ___ g ___ ___ t

N ___ ___ ___ ___ ber

S ___ ___ t ___ ___ ber

Now write the months here in the correct order.

1 ______________________

7 ______________________

2 ______________________

8 ______________________

3 ______________________

9 ______________________

4 ______________________

10 ______________________

5 ______________________

11 ______________________

6 ______________________

12 ______________________

Fill in the missing letters of the days of the week.

Th __ __ __ day

S __ __ day

Sa __ __ __ day

F __ __ day

T __ __ __ day

M __ __ day

W __ __ __ __ __ day

Now make two lists. In one list put the days in their correct order (the first one has been done for you). In the second list arrange the days in alphabetical order.

13 Correct order	14 Alphabetical order
Sunday	

Something's missing

Match the words with **apostrophes** with the longer versions.

Colour each pair using a different colour.

The short versions are called ***contractions****.*

For each contraction, write down the letters that have been missed out.

Find the adjectives

Look at this jumble of words and draw a circle round each of the **adjectives**. You should be able to find ten.

Adjectives are words which describe nouns.

tall river

actor night round

slow quick playground

white journey

thick jump

bald

tasty sweet

sing

athlete farm

road

dark

Think of a noun that each adjective could describe.

Animal crossword

The answers to this crossword are all animals, birds or insects.

ACROSS

1 This animal never forgets (8 letters).

5 Like a mouse, but bigger (3 letters).

7 A fierce, striped animal that lives in the jungle (5 letters).

8 An animal that human beings ride (5 letters).

DOWN

2 The king of the jungle (4 letters).

3 A bird that can repeat what you say (6 letters).

4 A small, hardworking insect (3 letters).

6 The tallest animal of all (7 letters).

Fill in the easy words first, and see if they give you any clues to the more difficult ones.

Where do I find it?

This is the **contents** page of a book about dinosaurs. After you have looked at it, answer the questions on the opposite page.

The world of dinosaurs

CONTENTS

1 Which two chapters would you look at if you wanted to find out about creatures who lived on the earth and in the sea before the dinosaurs?

2 If you wanted to find out which types of food dinosaurs liked, which page would you turn to?

3 Which chapter would you look at for information about dinosaur bones and fossils?

4 If you wanted to know why dinosaurs became extinct, which page would you turn to?

5 Which chapter would you look at if you wanted to find out about other creatures who lived on earth at the time of the dinosaurs?

6 In which section of the book would you find all the topics covered in the book listed in alphabetical order?

There was an old man...

Here are three poems written over a hundred years ago by Edward Lear.

There was an Old Man with a beard
Who said, 'It is just as I feared!
Two Owls and a Hen,
Four Larks and a Wren
Have all built their nests in my beard!'

There was an Old Man who said, 'How
Shall I flee from that horrible cow?
I will sit on this stile,
And continue to smile,
Which may soften the heart of that cow.'

There was an Old Man in a tree,
Who was horribly bored by a bee.
When they said, 'Does it buzz?'
He replied, 'Yes, it does!
It's a regular brute of a bee!'

Poems like this are called **limericks**. Can you see that the three poems have several things in common? Here are some questions to help you see how they are similar.

1. How many lines does each poem have? ____________________

2. Which lines are long and which lines are short?

____

3. Which lines rhyme? ____

4. How does each poem begin? ______________________________

5. Poems like this are also called **nonsense poems**. You can probably see why!

Now you know how limericks are made, why not try writing one yourself in the box below?

Group words

Try to sort the words below into pairs. You need to match each group word with the things that it describes. One has been done for you.

*Group words like **herd** and **swarm** are called **collective nouns**.*

A swarm

A herd

of flowers

A bunch

of people

A pack

of birds

A team

of bees

A fleet

of elephants

of ships

of footballers

of wolves

A crowd

A flock

A bunch of flowers ______________________

______________________ ______________________

______________________ ______________________

______________________ ______________________

Word hunt

Here are some words that all end with the letters **le**:

little muddle bottle puddle trouble cradle

Can you find these words hidden in the puzzle below?
You need to look down, across and diagonally.

l	n	b	t	k	t	s	c
p	l	b	r	v	u	w	r
u	i	h	o	g	f	p	a
d	t	n	u	t	p	q	d
d	t	k	b	v	t	u	l
l	l	w	l	d	o	l	e
e	e	x	e	n	l	e	e
m	u	d	d	l	e	b	c

*Can you think of other words that end in **le**?*

Why not make up your own word search?

Name the noun

Proper nouns like Wendy, Scotland and Concorde, always begin with a capital letter. They tell us the names of particular persons, places and things.

Common nouns like girl, country and aeroplane, don't begin with a capital letter unless the word is at the beginning of a sentence.

Here are ten nouns. Decide if each one is a proper noun or a common noun and put it in the correct column.

queen

chicken

michael

wembley

europe

sea

paris

radio

car

wales

1 Common nouns

2 Proper nouns

Now find the nouns in this piece of writing.
There are ten different ones altogether.

There are many rivers in England. Probably the most famous is called the Thames. It flows through many towns and villages and passes under many bridges. Before it reaches the sea it flows through London, where it passes the Houses of Parliament and the Tower of London.

Decide what sort of noun they are and write them in the correct box.

3 **Common nouns**

4 **Proper nouns**

House crossword

In this crossword the answers are all to do with houses.

ACROSS

2 You open this to get in (4 letters).

4 This lets in light (6 letters).

5 Where you might park a car (6 letters).

7 A room where you sleep (7 letters).

DOWN

1 Without these you couldn't get up to some of the rooms (6 letters).

2 A path to the house for cars (5 letters).

3 This keeps the rain out (4 letters).

6 Outside the house, where you might play in the summer (6 letters).

Make up a crossword of your own using school as the theme.

Not quite right

Ten **spelling mistakes** have been underlined in this story. Write out the words correctly in the spaces at the bottom of the page.

A new gurl strated at my school today. Her naim is Shareem and she is in my class. Our teacher Miss Jones sat Shareem at my tabel. Miss Jones said, 'We must make Shareem feel at home.' David White said, 'Do you meen feel at school, Miss?' Shareem laghed and Miss Jones said, 'Are you being cheeky, David?'

David said, 'Sorry, Miss.'

At playtime I asked Shareem if she would like to play skiping. Shareem said, 'Thank you, Liz, but I really like playing football.' Soun we were all playing football and Shareem scored to goals. My freinds and I cheered. We can't wait to play football again tomorrow!

Pronouns

I, you, he, she, it, we and they are words we use instead of nouns. They are called **pronouns**. Me, him, her and them are pronouns too.

Put the missing pronoun in these sentences.

1 Andy asked for his pencil back so I gave it to _________.

2 When the teacher found Jenny's lost jumper she knew it

belonged to _________.

3 I chose the cherry lollipop because _________ was red.

4 When Calum and Harry got home _________ went outside to play.

5 The bus went before we got to the bus stop. 'I knew _________ would be late!' my mum said crossly.

6 Dad looked tired out when _________ got home from work.

7 "Don't shout at me! _________ don't like it."

8 "If I'm good, will _________ get me a present?" I asked my mum.

Dictionary quiz

Here is another page from a **dictionary**, with some questions about it on the opposite page.

This dictionary tells you what a female actor is called.

activity *noun* **1** the condition of a lot of action; **2** something that is done, especially for interest

actor feminine **actress** *noun* a person who acts a part in a play or film

actual *adjective* real and clear; **actually** *adverb*

add *verb* **1** to put a number, etc with another number; **2** to say something extra; **addition** *noun*; **additional** *adjective*

address *noun* the number of the building, name of the street and town, etc, where a person lives or works

adjective *noun* a word that describes something

admire *verb* to think of with pleasure and respect; to have a good opinion of something or somebody; **admiration** *noun*

admit *verb* **(admitted) 1** to allow somebody to enter; to let in; **2** to confess; **admission** *noun*

adult *noun* **1** a fully grown person, especially a person over 18; **2** a fully grown animal or bird; **adult** *adjective*

advantage *noun* something that may help you to be successful or to get something you want; **advantageous** *adjective*

adventure *noun* an exciting and often dangerous journey, activity, etc; **adventurous** *adjective*

adverb *noun* a word which tells you how, when, or where something is done

advertise *verb* to make something known to a lot of people; **advertisement** *noun*

advice *noun* a suggestion from one person to another on how that other should act

Some nouns come from verbs (like advertisement and advertise).

1 Is the word add a noun or a verb? ____________________

2 How many different meanings does the dictionary give for the word add? ____________________

3 What noun comes from the verb admire? ____________________

4 According to the dictionary, how old is an adult? ________________

5 Here are picture clues for three more words beginning with the letter a. Write each word next to its picture, and try to explain what each word means. Use a dictionary if you get stuck!

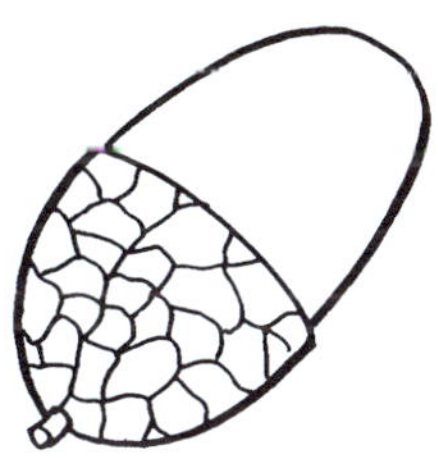

____

____

____

____

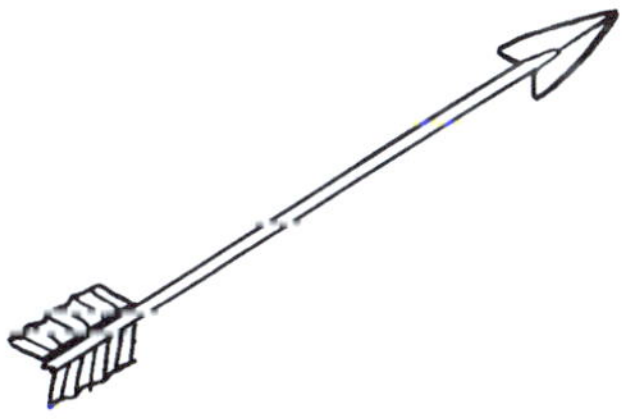

____

____

Find the conjunctions

Draw a circle round each of the **conjunctions** in this list.
You should be able to find nine.

although

cat

shiny

until

strong

because

roof

so

fresh

string

if

while

but

magnificent

when

purple

shoe

and

large

Conjunctions are joining words that connect two parts of a sentence.

Now choose words from the ones you have circled to go in the spaces in these sentences. Only use each word once.

The first one has been done for you.

1 We met Aunt Mary ___when___ we went to the shops.

2 I lived in that house __________ I was six, then we moved here.

3 The dog was hungry __________ I gave him a biscuit.

4 I like playing dominoes __________ my sister prefers snakes and ladders.

5 I went to bed early __________ I was tired.

6 I went to the pantomime __________ my friend Charles went as well.

7 My brother is very good at gymnastics __________ he is only seven years old.

8 We had a drink __________ we were waiting.

9 We will catch the bus __________ we hurry.

Look it up!

Here is part of the **contents page** of a book about Europe. When you have looked at it, answer the questions on the opposite page.

1 What is the title of the chapter that has information about Wales?

2 Which page would you turn to for information about Denmark?

3 What is the number of the chapter that has information about France?

4 Which page does the chapter that includes Spain begin on?

5 If you wanted to compare Holland and Sweden, which two pages would you turn to?

6 Hungary is a country in Central Europe. Which page would you turn to for information about it?

Time to pause

Put a full stop when you have finished saying something.

Write in **full stops** and **capital letters** to make two sentences each time.

Put a capital letter at the beginning of a sentence.

1 We went to the park yesterday. It was nice and sunny.

2 many other people were there as well I saw my friend Charlie

3 Charlie asked me to play football with him I agreed and we had a really good game

4 after that we had a picnic Mum had brought some food and drink

5 we had ice creams as well they were nice and cool

6 charlie and his sister shared the picnic with us they thought it was great

7 then Charlie and his sister had to go it was so enjoyable being in the park Mum and I decided to stay

8 we walked over to the lake we fed the ducks some scraps of bread

9 we saw a beautiful swan we had never noticed him in the lake before

10 finally we went home for our tea it had been a perfect day

Commas are a way of marking pauses in a piece of writing. Add a comma to each of these sentences.

Put the comma where you might pause if you read the sentence out loud.

11 I put on the red dress the one that was my favourite.

12 Mum said I should put on another dress so I chose my blue one.

13 It went better with my new shoes the ones with the blue bows.

14 She said I looked very pretty even prettier than I did in the red dress.

Commas are also used to separate the items in a list. Add commas to these sentences.

You need commas after every item in a list except the last two.

15 When I arrived at the party Emily Ellen Lizzie and Kevin were already there.

16 We ate ice creams jelly cakes and crisps.

17 We played snap tiddlywinks I-spy and dominoes.

18 We also danced watched television and played in the garden.

Sorting words

Here is part of a book about dinosaurs. Read it, then answer the questions on the opposite page.

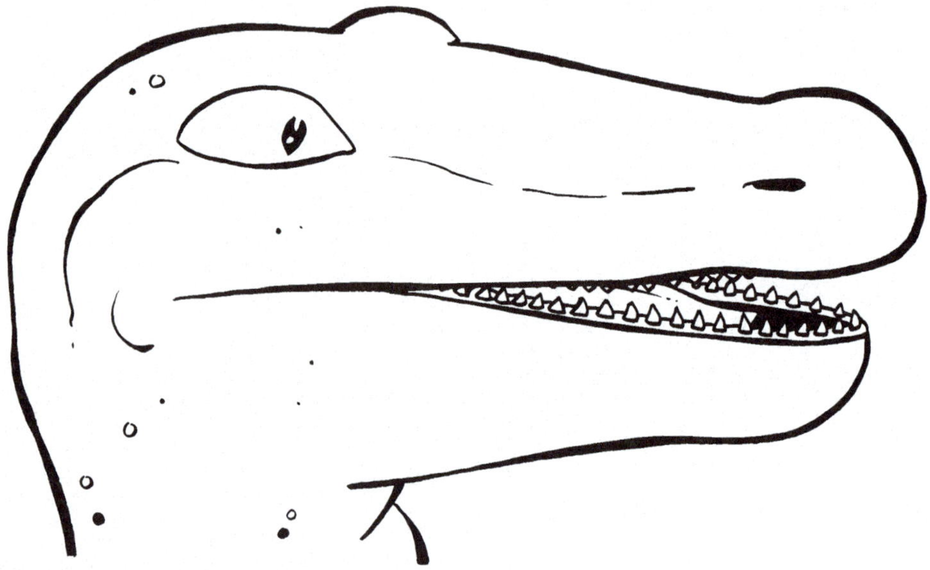

Some dinosaurs had huge eyes. We know this because scientists have looked carefully at dinosaur skeletons. Their eyes were large so they could hunt more easily. They had good eyesight. In some cases their eyes were at the sides of their heads. This meant they could see all around them.

Some dinosaurs had huge nostrils as well and were probably able to smell food or other animals from a long way away.

We think of dinosaurs as fierce creatures, but maybe some of them were not. Many dinosaurs ate plants, not other animals. Perhaps these were gentle creatures, although some people find it hard to imagine a friendly dinosaur!

Can you find the following in the passage you have just read?

Five **nouns**
Five **verbs**
Five **conjunctions**
Five **adjectives**

Conjunctions are joining words that connect two parts of a sentence.

To help you get started, one of each has already been found for you.

1 **Nouns**

dinosaurs

2 **Verbs**

looked

3 **Conjunctions**

because

4 **Adjectives**

huge

What do you mean?

On the left are some words from a dictionary. On the right are their **meanings**, but they are in the wrong order. Draw lines to join each word to its correct meaning.

lemon	1	a powerful machine used for pushing heavy objects, earth etc. out of the way
knight	2	a large yellow fruit that is like an orange but is sour
bulldozer	3	a person in an army
soldier	4	**1** a type of fruit like an orange but with a light yellow skin and sour juice; **2** a light bright yellow colour
tractor	5	a man given the title 'Sir' by the king or queen of Great Britain
grapefruit	6	a powerful motor vehicle used for pulling farm machinery or other heavy objects

The right choice

Here is more information from a **thesaurus**. You would find these words listed if you looked up parcel, journey, hill and cut.

parcel – packet, bundle, bag, box, package

journey – trip, outing, tour, drive, ride, flight, cruise, voyage, walk

hill – bank, hillside, mountain

cut – chop, slice, carve, saw, mow

Choose the best word from those above for the sentences below.

1 I bought a _______________ of biscuits at the shop.

2 I asked the baker to _______________ the bread.

3 Before we have dinner I must _______________ the meat.

4 We had a picnic on the _______________ of the river.

5 The aeroplane landed after a very long _______________ .

6 It was only a short _______________ to the cinema so we did not go by car.

What do you say?

Here are some words that can be used instead of **said**:

asked shouted replied whispered agreed

Choose words from this list to put in the spaces below.

1 'How are you?' the old lady _____________ .

2 'I'm very well, thank you,' Tommy _____________ .

3 'Let me tell you a secret,' she _____________ . 'Come closer so nobody else can hear.'

4 'All right,' Tommy _____________ as he moved towards her.

5 To Tommy's surprise the old lady suddenly yelled at the top of her voice. 'You're standing on my foot!' she _____________ .

Here are some more words that can take the place of said:

cried called groaned begged gasped answered

Can you find these words hidden in the puzzle below?
You need to look down and across.

Try using these words in some sentences of your own.

a	r	t	o	n	v	c	a
g	a	s	p	e	d	a	n
r	w	x	a	r	s	l	t
o	y	n	i	b	m	l	e
a	n	s	w	e	r	e	d
n	o	u	d	g	p	d	q
e	r	l	a	g	h	b	s
d	m	f	a	e	s	g	h
c	r	i	e	d	a	l	p

Using different words for said makes your writing more interesting.

Space crossword

In this crossword the answers are all to do with space. The clues are on the opposite page.

ACROSS

1 On a clear night the sky is full of these (5 letters).

3 The planet we live on (5 letters).

4 At night it's the biggest thing we can see in the sky (4 letters).

6 If beings ever visit us from other worlds, they may travel in a flying __________ (6 letters).

8 'Star __________' is the name of a television programme and a set of films about space travel (4 letters).

DOWN

1 Where heat and light come from (3 letters).

2 Creatures from space (6 letters).

5 Anywhere that is a long way from Earth is part of __________ space (5 letters).

7 If you went to the moon you might go there in one of these (6 letters).

Begin and end

Make new words from these words by taking away either the first few letters or the last few letters. One has been done for you.

*If you take away the first few letters you are taking away a **prefix**.*

*If you take away the last few letters you are taking away a **suffix**.*

1	unusual	usual
2	disagree	______
3	useless	______
4	careful	______
5	return	______
6	mistake	______
7	scarcely	______
8	nonsense	______
9	kindness	______
10	prehistoric	______

Answers and Hints

In some instances there may be more than one possible answer so you may need to check that the answer your child has given is reasonable. As long as your child's answer makes sense and has shown they understand the question, you should mark it right. Sometimes the question will ask them to fill in facts about themselves, or to express an opinion, or to create their own piece of work. You may want to judge your child's effort for yourself, but please remember that encouragement is always more helpful than criticism.

PAGE 6
plurals with es: foxes, pushes, benches, coaches, wishes, glasses, boxes, gases, fizzes **plurals with s:** zoos, drinks, smiles, socks, baths

PAGE 7
synonyms pairs (any order): cheerful–happy, country–nation, enquire–ask, lofty–tall, complete–whole, wrong–incorrect, pretty–attractive, sad–miserable

PAGE 8
nouns: astronaut, saucer, computer, Wendy, house, London, penguin, zoo, aeroplane, grass Being able to identify parts of speech (nouns, adjectives, etc.) will help your child in understanding and applying the rules of grammar.

PAGE 9
Word searches encourage your child to look for groups of letters and increase familiarity with spelling patterns.

h	e	r	n	a	r	b	s
m	p	r	m	c	n	i	t
w	u	u	o	g	d	r	i
e	r	h	e	a	r	d	r
r	r	c	k	i	f	u	r
e	h	u	z	s	s	b	e
b	t	m	s	w	o	r	d

PAGE 10
2 (missing words) bat, ban (or bit) 3 dot, cot 4 tame, lame 5 send, bend (or sent) 6 lake, like (or lane) 7 pan, pal 8 wand (or bind), band 9 talk, tale

PAGE 11
2 having 3 making 4 laughing 5 calling 6 taking 7 snowing 8 raining 9 trying 10 smiling

PAGES 12 & 13
Try to help your child understand how a dictionary works, and encourage your child to make regular use of one. It is best to choose one specially designed for children. 1 noun 2 three 3 cry 4 The answer your child gives will depend on the dictionary they are using, but missing words could include cream, creature, creep, crew and cricket. Does your child understand why these words come between crawl and cried? 5 You will need to check your child's definitions are accurate and show that they understand the meaning of the words.

PAGES 14 & 15
Check your child has used the events in the pictures to fill in Sally's diary. Many children enjoy keeping diaries and the regular writing practice helps to develop writing skills.

PAGE 16
verbs: sew, listen, find, swim, collect, draw, grow, juggle, ask, throw

PAGE 17
Although most verbs can be changed to the past tense simply by adding ed, many cannot. Help your child become familiar with these more difficult verbs and their spellings. 2 see, saw 3 think, thought 4 keep, kept 5 throw, threw 6 go, went 7 know, knew 8 grow, grew 9 wake, woke 10 do, did

PAGES 18 & 19
Early use of a thesaurus is encouraged within the National Curriculum guidelines. Like a dictionary, a thesaurus is an invaluable reference tool and it is important your child learns how to use one. 1 three 2 motorway 3 street 4 envelope flap 5 catflap 6 pumpkin, table and desk 7 bedside lamp 8 halloween

PAGE 20
A knowledge of prefixes and suffixes is an aid to spelling and also helps a child to guess more accurately at the meanings of unfamiliar words. 1 dis(appear) 2 re(do) 3 anti(clockwise) 4 non(sense) 5 pre(historic) 6 mis(placed)

PAGE 21
use: useful, useless **sad:** sadly **proud:** proudly **hope:** hopeful, hopeless **quick:** quickly **slow:** slowly **nice:** nicely **head:** headless **loud:** loudly **care:** careful, careless **clear:** clearly The words useless, hopeful, hopeless, careful and careless can all have the letters 'ly' added to them.

PAGE 22
matched pairs: can't–cannot, won't–will not, don't–do not, I've–I have, you'd–you had

PAGE 23
2 basketball 3 airport 4 footprint 5 shoelace 6 windmill

PAGE 24
1 helmet 2 soup 3 tower 4 hat 5 stream 6 invite

PAGE 25
antonyms pairs (any order): rude–polite, short–tall, over–under, upper–lower, nice–nasty

PAGE 26
2 Doctor Doolittle 3 Dumbo 4 Hercules 5 James and the Giant Peach 6 Snow White 7 Star Trek 8 Treasure Island

PAGE 27
message reads: The sweets are behind the clock. Eat this message when you have read it!

PAGES 28 & 29
Check your child has spelt the months and days correctly throughout. 1 January 2 February 3 March 4 April 5 May 6 June 7 July 8 August 9 September 10 October 11 November 12 December 13 (correct order) Sunday, Monday, Tuesday, Wednesday, Thursday, Friday, Saturday 14 (alphabetical order) Friday, Monday, Saturday, Sunday, Thursday, Tuesday, Wednesday

PAGE 30
matched pairs: it's–it is, you're–you are, you've–you have, we'll–we will, I'm–I am

PAGE 31
adjectives: tall, round, slow, quick, white, thick, bald, tasty, sweet, dark

PAGES 32 & 33
across: (1) elephant, (5) rat, (7) tiger, (8) horse
down: (2) lion, (3) parrot, (4) ant, (6) giraffe

PAGES 34 & 35
1 chapters 1 and 2 2 page 25 3 chapter 9 4 page 47 5 chapter 7 6 the index

PAGES 36 & 37
1 five 2 (long lines) 1, 2 & 5; (short lines) 3 & 4 3 lines 1, 2 & 5 rhyme with each other; lines 3 & 4 also rhyme 4 There was an Old Man... 5 Writing their own poetry encourages children to expand their vocabulary and think about sounds and associations of words. Writing a limerick will help them think about rhythm and rhyming words. Be generous in your appraisal of their limerick. Before they start, you may need to talk about what ideas your child might use. Why not have a go at writing one yourself? (This is a good way to appreciate the difficulties your child may encounter!)

PAGE 38
collective nouns (any order): A herd of elephants, A swarm of bees, A team of footballers, A crowd of people, A fleet of ships, A flock of birds, A pack of wolves

PAGE 39

l	n	b	t	k	t	s	c
p	l	b	r	v	u	w	r
u	i	h	o	g	f	p	a
d	t	n	u	t	p	q	d
d	t	k	b	v	t	u	l
l	l	w	l	d	o	l	e
e	e	x	e	n	l	e	e
m	u	d	d	l	e	b	c

PAGES 40 & 41
1 (any order) queen, chicken, sea, radio, car 2 (any order) Paris, Michael, Wembley, Europe, Wales 3 (any order) rivers, towns, villages, bridges, sea 4 (any order) England, Thames, London, Houses of Parliament, Tower of London

PAGES 42 & 43
across: (2) door, (4) window, (5) garage, (7) bedroom
down: (1) stairs, (2) drive, (3) roof, (6) garden

PAGE 44
correct spellings (in the order in which they appear): girl, started, name, table, mean, laughed, skipping, soon, two, friends

PAGE 45
Your child may have used different pronouns to complete some of the sentences; mark them correct if they make sense. 1 him 2 her 3 it 4 they 5 we 6 he 7 I 8 you

PAGES 46 & 47
1 a verb 2 two 3 admiration 4 over 18 5 Check that your child's definitions (for acorn, apple, arrow) are appropriate and make sense.

PAGE 48
conjunctions: although, until, because, so, if, but, while, when, and

PAGE 49
Your child may have used the conjunctions in different places to complete some of the sentences. Check that they have used each one once only and that the sentences make sense. 2 until 3 so 4 but 5 because 6 and 7 although 8 while 9 if

PAGES 50 & 51
1 United Kingdom and Ireland 2 page 59 3 chapter 7 4 page 89 5 pages 36 and 53 6 page 82

PAGES 52 & 53
2 Many other people were there as well. I saw my friend Charlie. 3 Charlie asked me to play football with him. I agreed and we had a really good game. 4 After that we had a picnic. Mum had brought some food and drink. 5 We had ice creams as well. They were nice and cool. 6 Charlie and his sister shared the picnic with us. They thought it was great. 7 Then Charlie and his sister had to go. It was so enjoyable being in the park Mum and I decided to stay. 8 We walked over to the lake. We fed the ducks some scraps of bread. 9 We saw a beautiful swan. We had never noticed him on the lake before. 10 Finally we went home for our tea. It had been a perfect day. 11 I put on the red dress, the one that was my favourite. 12 Mum said I should put on another dress, so I chose my blue one. 13 It went better with my new shoes, the ones with the blue bows. 14 She said I looked very pretty, even prettier than I did in the red dress. 15 When I arrived at the party Emily, Ellen, Lizzie and Kevin were already there. 16 We ate ice creams, jelly, cakes and crisps. 17 We played snap, tiddlywinks, I-spy and dominoes. 18 We also danced, watched television and played in the garden.

PAGES 54 & 55
You may need to remind your child that nouns are the words we use to name things, verbs are the words we use to describe actions ('doing words') and adjectives are words that describe nouns. 1 nouns (any four from this list): eyes, scientists, skeletons, eyesight, sides, heads, nostrils, food, animals, way, plants, creatures, people 2 verbs (any four): had, know, were, hunt, meant, could, see, able, smell, think, ate, find, imagine 3 conjunctions (any four): so, and, or, but, although 4 adjectives (any four): large, good, long, fierce, many, gentle, friendly

PAGE 56
The definitions for grapefruit and lemon show a fairly subtle difference. You may want to talk through the differences with your child and point out the clues - e.g. a grapefruit is described as being large; lemon is described as the name of a colour. 1 bulldozer 2 grapefruit 3 soldier 4 lemon 5 knight 6 tractor

PAGE 57
1 packet 2 slice 3 carve 4 bank 5 flight 6 walk

PAGES 58 & 59
1 asked 2 replied 3 whispered 4 agreed 5 shouted

a	r	t	o	n	v	c	a
g	a	s	p	e	d	a	n
r	w	x	a	r	s	l	t
o	y	n	i	b	m	l	e
a	n	s	w	e	r	e	d
n	o	u	d	g	p	d	q
e	r	l	a	g	h	b	s
d	m	f	a	e	s	g	h
c	r	i	e	d	a	l	p

PAGES 60 & 61
across: (1) stars, (3) earth, (4) moon, (6) saucer, (8) Trek
down: (1) sun, (2) aliens, (5) outer, (7) rocket

PAGE 62
2 agree 3 use (or less) 4 care 5 turn 6 take 7 scarce 8 sense 9 kind 10 historic